Beautiful Places

THE TIMELESS BEAUTY
OF SOUTH CAROLINA STATE PARKS

South Carolina
State Parks

Discovering this idyllic place,
we find ourselves filled
with a yearning to linger here,
where time stands still
and beauty overwhelms.

—*Author unknown*

Beautiful Places

THE TIMELESS BEAUTY
OF SOUTH CAROLINA STATE PARKS

Chad Prosser

Photography by jon o. holloway

Parks History by Cal Harrison

Foreword by Rudy Mancke

Published by the South Carolina
Department of Parks, Recreation & Tourism

Mark Sanford
Governor

Chad Prosser
Director

Corporate Partners: FUJIFILM Manufacturing U.S.A., Inc. and
BMW Manufacturing Co.

The images presented in this book were captured using digital media,
FUJIFILM film media such as Velvia 100F, Velvia 50F, Neopan 100 Acros,
and for one photo, a FinePix F-30 camera. High-quality FUJIFILM presensitized
printing plates were used to print the book to assure that the integrity of
the images was maintained. Both the film and printing plates were gladly
donated by FUJIFILM Manufacturing U.S.A., Inc.

Library of Congress Control Number: 2008928486
International Standard Book Number: 978-0-9798758-0-9
Editor: Gwen Davenport
Art Director: Jim Reel

All paper used for this book is Elemental Chlorine Free (ECF).

Contents

Acknowledgments

The magnificent beauty of South Carolina has inspired poets, sculptors, scientists and everyday philosophers. Hopefully this book will give you a tempting glimpse of the inspiration to be found in the 47 South Carolina State Parks, repository for many of our state's most-prized natural, historic and cultural resources.

These parks are available to us today because of the forward-thinking vision of prior generations—leaders both public and private who acted in their time to conserve our state's dearest resources, creating a connection with generations they would never know through the enduring strands of nature, culture and heritage. Many men labored in the Civilian Conservation Corps, some sacrificing life and limb, to construct our state parks. Today, the men and women of the State Park Service continue with the same dedication making our state parks a source of pride for South Carolina and a resource of renewal for all park visitors. We thank them.

Many individuals and organizations contributed to the success of this project. Of special note are: BMW and FUJIFILM, both companies, as South Carolina corporate citizens, have been long-standing supporters of South Carolina State Parks through this project and others; jon o. holloway, Cal Harrison and Chad Prosser; South Carolina Department of Parks, Recreation & Tourism, including State Park Service Director Phil Gaines, Beverly Shelley, Gwen Davenport, Amy Duffy, Justin Hancock and Lou Fontana; the bounce agency; and all friends and supporters of South Carolina State Parks.

A Note From the Author

As father of two young boys, I've watched the wonder of children as they encounter the slow-motion magic of a loggerhead sea turtle, the haunting mystery of Atalaya Castle and the sprawling roots of an oak tree that greeted Spanish explorers as Europeans discovered our great country.

The incredible vista from Caesars Head, the upstate hills of lush, Irish green, and the crashing, splashing, tumble-and-rumble of Raven Cliff Falls all wake us to the call of nature.

I fear the loss of these natural wonders. I fear the priorities of our time. This book is my argument against life lived too fast. I'm grateful for the state parks of South Carolina, the professionals who sustain them, and the people who fund their existence.

There is no substitute for natural beauty. The darkening of sky at sunset, the breeze coming off the ocean, the unexpected cry of an osprey—it's moments like these that make us feel human. I have no other word for it.

By purchasing this book you've helped to ensure that future generations will be able to drink from the well of nature's dark beauty. This is the mission of the South Carolina State Park Service. It is a daily passion for us.

Our parks are owned by the public, but less than one-quarter of our budget comes from state coffers. It's only through the support of people like you that we're able to reach out and connect America's people to parks.

Population growth and environmental challenges threaten the preservation of our parks as never before.

Thank you for buying the book. The next step is to visit the parks.

You'll find us standing at the entrance, waiting for you to arrive.

You're going to be glad you came, I promise.

Chad Prosser

P.S. If you worry as I do and would like to conserve and improve our parks, visit **www.BeautifulPlacesAlliance.org**, or call 1-800-471-4064 to learn about the different ways you can help.

Beautiful Places
A L L I A N C E

"Never doubt that a small group of thoughtful committed citizens can change the world; indeed, that is the only thing that ever has."
— *Margaret Mead.* Courtesy of The Institute for Intercultural Studies, Inc., New York.

Foreword

The people of South Carolina have always had a strong connection with the land. Natural resources have been the basis for our livelihood, providing food, water, air, shelter, recreation and more. The fabric of our lives and the unique heritage that is South Carolina come from those intricate relationships between humans and their environment.

Over time, people began to see the importance of protecting and caring for special places in the state. That concern led to the establishment of a state parks system 75 years ago.

On this anniversary, it is appropriate to look back and see how those parks came to be and how they have changed over the years. Parks have become a part of the very heritage they were meant to protect. They are treasures that serve as a long legacy for the future, and they are a wonderful mix of history and natural history, reflecting the diversity found within the state.

This book gives the reader a look at the history, as well as a photographic glimpse of all 47 state park properties that spread across the state, from the mountains to the sea.

Let me remind you that state parks are just as important now as they have ever been. Let me challenge you to support them in every way you can and never to take them for granted. I encourage you to enjoy and learn from this book, but don't stop there. Go, see and experience these special places for yourself.

Rudy Mancke
Naturalist

A lifelong naturalist, Rudy Mancke calls Spartanburg, South Carolina, his hometown. Mancke has spent his career enthusiastically sharing his love of the outdoors. For 25 years, he was host to South Carolina Educational TV's *NatureScene*, a nationally syndicated show which explored first the state then global destinations. Mancke has served as a teacher, Curator of Natural History at the South Carolina State Museum, and Director of Science and Nature Programming at SCETV. Mancke continues to spread his passion for the natural world as Distinguished Lecturer in Natural History at the University of South Carolina. He currently hosts *NatureNotes* on SCETV Radio.

History & Legacy

Table Rock, December 1935

A Spirit of Conservation

The vision for South Carolina's first state park was unveiled in January 1934 in a meeting hall packed with citizens from Cheraw, a small town near the state's northeastern border. Cheraw State Park would demonstrate how the science of conservation could transform worn-out cotton farmland into a shining example of the state's natural beauty. *The Cheraw Chronicle* heralded the park as a way to "establish Cheraw as the Gateway City of South Carolina." The park, expected to draw hundreds of thousands of visitors from across the country, would "stand in our midst as a perfectly planned living symbol of beauty." The meeting kicked off a fund-raising drive throughout Chesterfield County. Even in the depths of the Great Depression, more than 250 members of the community, including children who donated nickels and dimes, raised $5,326.32 for the new park. The money was used to buy 706 acres off U.S. 1 chosen by the state forester and representatives of the Civilian Conservation Corps (CCC). In the summer of 1934, South Carolina launched its multi-million dollar experiment in "recreational forestry."

A decade earlier it would have been unheard of to call in the federal government to develop state parks, but South Carolina was in crisis. Forest lands were badly cut over. Replanting and soil conservation techniques were nonexistent. Despite an ominous report that predicted the disappearance of the state's forests by 1927, the General Assembly resisted efforts to create the state Commission of Forestry for five years. Forestry and conservation were viewed as Northern, elitist movements that ran counter to the pro-business environment permeating the New South. During a heated debate in 1922, the Senate refused to invite noted conservationist Gifford Pinchot to speak on the topic. But that arrogance stimulated a grassroots movement. Women's Clubs and Audubon Society members statewide were outraged.

Mrs. E.A. Donovant of Edgefield warned that the state was "in constant danger of affecting our rainfall, our water power and our water supply by the wanton waste of our forests, and like the Chinese we are going to find ourselves—no, not ourselves, but something dearer, our children—on the world's charity." The outgoing governor convened a forestry conference. Soon the cause of forest conservation was taken up by Kiwanis Clubs, and in 1927 lawmakers created the state Forestry Commission, an all-volunteer board with only one employee—and no funding. The newly appointed commission asked for help from the federal government. With the aid of the U.S. Forest Service, the commission found its first state forester, Lewis E. Staley, in Pennsylvania.

The state's new forestry program began in 1928 with a $4,000 appropriation by the legislature and donations by the commission chairman, Florence lumberman Horace L. Tilghman. It was hoped that an educational campaign would help save the state's timber industry. Then came the Great Depression.

From Bad to Worse

South Carolina's economy was already struggling in October 1929 when the stock market crashed on Wall Street. Orders for textile goods ground to a halt. The bottom fell out of cotton prices. The per capita income throughout the Southeast was $250—less than half the national average. Over the next four years, 11,000 banks would fail nationwide. The national unemployment rate climbed and eventually peaked at 24.9 percent in 1933, but exceeded 30 percent in more than one-third of South Carolina's counties.

Throughout the early 1930s, a prolonged drought plagued the Midwest. Powerful dust storms stripped tons of topsoil from the prairie states. South Carolina had its own scare during the dry fall of 1931 when rampant woods fires across the Lowcountry drove tourists from roads, rerouted airmail and even prevented ships from entering Charleston Harbor. A forest protection plan calling for the construction of fire towers and firebreaks was developed for the state's coastal region, but with no state funding, the plan sat on a shelf—until things began to change in Washington.

New Deal for South Carolina

Franklin D. Roosevelt swept the Democrats into office in 1932, pledging in his nomination speech to employ one million men "for the reforestation of vast areas." Roosevelt put 250,000 World War I veterans and younger men to work that

BEN MEEKS:
FATHER OF STATE PARKS

The son of a Baptist minister, Ben S. Meeks was a businessman with a conservationist's heart. Born in New York where he attended Colgate University, Meeks worked as a commercial agent for the Atlantic Coastline Railroad in Florence. He worked closely with Horace L. Tilghman, a Florence lumberman who shipped thousands of tons of lumber on Atlantic Coastline cars. When South Carolina's timber industry was on the verge of collapse in the 1920s, both men were alarmed. Meeks, a lifelong Kiwanis Club member, appealed to the state board and eventually every Kiwanis Club in the state to lobby the legislature for help. Both men were appointed to the newly formed Commission of Forestry—Tilghman, the first chairman, succeeded by Meeks, who served for more than two decades. Meeks, who was involved in the development of a Florence city park, traveled to Washington as early as 1929 to speak to National Park Service officials about building parks in South Carolina.

Two years later, the commission hired a new state forester, Homer Arthur "H.A." Smith, a Pennsylvania native who, like Meeks, saw recreation as a way to demonstrate forest conservation. With the backing of President Roosevelt in 1933, Meeks and Smith traversed the state over the next eight years to acquire land and oversee the program. The parks were seen as a huge success. Smith was elected president of the Association of State Foresters and later hired by the Tennessee Valley Authority. By the 1940s, however, the parks had become a political liability for Meeks, who was unceremoniously replaced. "He read in the newspaper one day that the governor had accepted his resignation—and that was how he found out," according to his son, Spencer Meeks.

year under the new Civilian Conservation Corps. State forestry commissioners traveled to Washington in 1933 with a plan for the federal government to manage its forest conservation program in 13 coastal counties. Roosevelt personally approved the plan, and South Carolina was allocated 17 CCC camps. Initially employing nearly 3,500 men, the CCC erected 48 fire towers and cleared 1,200 miles of firebreak.

In May 1933, the legislature gave the commission the authority to administer State Forest Parks. Within months, money was raised to buy land for Cheraw State Park, and by June 1934 several hundred enrollees of CCC Camp 445 set up tents and began building four barracks, a dining hall, a recreation hall and separate quarters for officers and state park supervisors. The next year, the federal government purchased 7,361 acres adjacent to Cheraw State Park and set aside another 6,100 acres next to the Kings Mountain Revolutionary War Battlefield as demonstration sites for recreational programs. Communities across South Carolina came forward with plans for inclusion in the program. "One fire tower was worth more than a thousand talks before Kiwanis Clubs," noted state forester H.A. Smith. "The people wanted CCC camps, and they wanted parks. There is an ever-growing demand for recreational facilities."

Economic motives fueled many of the proposed parks. Along the coast, land donated by Myrtle Beach Farms and the Edisto Company was expected to boost the state's fledgling tourism industry. Beaufort County donated 5,000 acres on Hunting Island for a state park to speed the construction of a long hoped for bridge to its barrier islands. The city of Columbia, celebrating its 150th anniversary, donated 1,400 acres acquired by its Sesquicentennial Commission. Charleston donated Givhans Ferry on the Edisto River and the city of Greenville donated Paris Mountain, the former site of the city's water reservoir. Greenville and Pickens County also donated Table Rock, a commanding granite outcropping already used as a recreational area for the Upstate. Small rural counties including Sumter, Oconee, Lee, Barnwell and Chester also set aside land for the program.

"It Taught Me a Lot About Living"

CCC camps sprouted from the dirt across the state, and nearly 500,000 young men lived and worked in the new parks. Fifteen companies of white men and eight companies of black men—living in segregated areas—earned $30 a month, with a mandatory $22 sent home to their families. "That was the difference between starvation and having something to eat for my family," recalled Greenville County native James Shepherd.

With food, clothing and shelter provided, the men performed backbreaking work—clearing land, planting trees and building dams, roads and buildings. They attended educational classes and received training in typewriting, forestry, landscaping, mechanics and electrification. The public was so enamored with the CCC that an estimated 70 percent of enrollees found jobs after leaving the corps. "It's like being in the army," said Woodrow Coggins, who joined the CCC in 1934. "You wouldn't want to do it again, but you wouldn't take anything for the experience. It taught me a lot about living."

Myrtle Beach State Park opened to the public with great fanfare on July 1, 1936. Thousands of visitors strolled the park's two-story beachfront bathhouse and boardwalk. Approximately one new park a year opened its gates over the next six years. In eight years, the CCC planted more than 56 million trees and built 900 bridges, 129 lookout towers and 16 state parks. CCC workers built cabins, picnic shelters and staff residences throughout the parks—many of which are still standing. As jobs became more plentiful and as attention focused on war mobilization, support for the CCC waned and funding was cut in 1942.

In 1937, the first year records were kept, an estimated 387,000 people visited the parks. Sites were selected to ensure at least one state park would be within 50 miles of every resident of the state. Summer day camps introduced school children to swimming, archery, music, dancing, nature hikes and crafts. Weekends at the parks were packed with cabin renters, swimmers and group outings. Soon, the number of picnickers was reported to surpass swimmers.

The Civilian Conservation Corps statue at the entrance to Oconee State Park was dedicated in 2001 as a tribute to the CCC workers who built many of the state's park facilities and structures across the country.

The World War II "Invasion"

Despite their popularity, the parks almost didn't open in the summer of 1942, just six months after the United States entered World War II. "An attempt was made to stop operating the parks, but public clamor was too great, and the service which would be rendered to members of the armed forces was too evident," according to J.H. Gadsby, acting State Parks Director.

The state turned over its three coastal parks to the Army, Navy and Coast Guard for training camps. An estimated 100,000 military men visited the state parks between 1942 and 1943. British sailors, in port for repairs in Charleston, were regulars at Cheraw State Park's cabins more than 150 miles away.

At the end of the war in 1945, as the coastal parks reopened, more than 550,000 people visited the parks.

The Family Recreation Boom

During the peacetime economic boom, the birthrate began its steady rise and young families had more money and time for leisure. The workweek had fallen steadily from 60 hours at the turn of the century to 45 hours in the 1940s. Recreation was considered crucial to filling that extra time. Two-day weekends, paid vacations and national holidays gave families more time for weekend getaways. Cheap gasoline and improved highways boosted annual U.S. automobile production from nearly nonexistent during the war to seven million vehicles in 1950. State parks offered affordable family vacations that were in reach of nearly every South Carolina family.

To meet growing demands, park cabins and group camps were electrified in 1946. The state established two new parks in the 1940s—Santee State Park on the banks of Lake Marion and Croft State Park near Spartanburg.

Annual park attendance doubled to two million visitors statewide between 1946 and 1949, and reached the three million mark in 1951. Parking lots and picnic tables filled by noon in the summer months. Waiting lists for cabins grew long. Despite warnings by the Forestry Commission that facilities were "designed to carry a load of less than a million people," the state legislature was reluctant to increase spending on parks.

With no admission fees in the early years, the parks were expected to pay for themselves through rental fees for cabins, boats and recreational programs. In reality, without federal support, fees generated only about half of the cost to run the parks. The state was spending only about 12 cents per park visitor—40 percent less than the national average.

With premier facilities at Myrtle Beach and Table Rock receiving a lion's share of

From the beginning, families often ventured out to the new state parks for inexpensive family picnics such as in this 1938 photo taken at Table Rock State Park.

the funding, most parks were staffed by a park superintendent and a maintenance worker. Repairs to facilities were made with scavenged lumber and used hardware.

"We'd get buckets of bent nails that had to be hammered straight before we could use them," recalled Ray Sisk, a superintendent at Kings Mountain in the early 1960s. "Times were tough."

The need for funding prompted the Forestry Commission to add more park campsites in the 1950s. The parks reached out to communities with group camps and a radio show hosted by park rangers, "The World is Full of a Number of Wonderful Things," was broadcast by eight different radio stations.

As the popularity of family camping grew, fees helped sustain the parks. Other funding strategies brought mixed results. Boxes were installed near picnic tables to collect a 25-cent picnicking fee, but visitors at most parks were left on the honor system.

The state even experimented with leasing lots for private homes at one park. The Beach Village concept at Hunting Island caught on, leaving the park with 30 private lots carved out for private use. The lack of funding, already a sensitive issue among state legislative delegations, would soon prove to be a divisive issue for many South Carolina communities.

Two Races, Two Park Systems

Throughout the 1940s and 1950s, as the state actively promoted its parks, swimming pools and cabins, the divide between whites-only and blacks-only "Negro" parks became acutely apparent. Developed under the U.S. Supreme Court's longstanding "separate but equal" doctrine, only four of the 16 state parks planned during the 1930s included segregated areas for blacks.

Greenwood and Hunting Island state parks had separate entrances, facilities and swimming areas. Employees at Cheraw and Poinsett state parks managed nearby areas for blacks called Campbell's Pond and Mill Creek.

A 1948 study found that South Carolina led the Southeast in both the number and total acreage of state parks for blacks. But state officials, who stated that whites generated greater demand, made the development of "Negro" parks a low priority.

An extensive park for blacks, to be named Hickory Knob, was planned for the new Clarks Hill Lake on the Savannah River, but plans were shelved. Efforts to create a segregated area at Sesquicentennial State Park in Columbia failed. Meanwhile, the state added two new whites-only parks—Croft and Andrew Jackson. Black leaders decried the lack of recreational areas.

Tragedy at Pleasant Ridge

The controversy soon moved to the Upstate. An auditorium of whites in the Greenville area convinced the state to drop plans for a new park adjacent to Paris Mountain. Landowners of two other potential sites withdrew under pressure. The Forestry Commission bought an option to buy 340 acres near Pelzer. However, the General Assembly balked at the purchase at the close of its 1948 session, and the site was dropped.

It took the commission and the city of Greenville another 18 months to acquire a 300-acre site north of Greenville from the Enoree River Colored Baptist Association. The location of Pleasant Ridge State Park was a closely held secret until the 1950 summer season ended. Yet finding a site for the park was just part of the battle. Plans called for construction in phases over five years, but the Legislature provided only piecemeal funding and ultimately appropriated only two-thirds of the needed $95,000.

With the official opening still years away, area black families started visiting Pleasant Ridge in 1952. Two years later, with the park still lacking a bathhouse, camping area, waterfront, picnic shelter and drinking water system, black leaders were losing patience. A tragic accident on July 29, 1954—the drowning of three boys from a youth group boating on the lake—focused media attention on the debacle.

Citizens were shocked to learn the lake, built in 1951, had never been officially opened and staffed for the public. The lake was subsequently drained to prevent further tragedies. In an editorial, *The Greenville News* reporter Gil Rowland charged that the black community had been a victim of a "magnificent runaround." He urged readers to compare Pleasant Ridge with Paris Mountain State Park to decide whether blacks were receiving separate-but-equal opportunities. In the same newspaper, local black leader Dr. E.L. McPherson said many bear the blame for the tragedy at Pleasant Ridge but "my gripe is with the powers that be. Why, pray tell, in the years since the park has been purchased have not adequate funds been appropriated?"

The next month, state lawmakers earmarked $10,000 to complete the park, which finally opened in the spring of 1955. Attendance at Pleasant Ridge was moderate and never increased after integration because of its proximity to Table Rock and Paris Mountain parks. The controversial park remained in the state system for the next 27 years until it was deeded to Greenville County, which now operates it as a county park.

Brown vs. S.C. State Forestry Commission

Fear of desegregation dominated the political landscape of South Carolina in the 1950s and 1960s. In May 1955, six NAACP members from Charleston wrote letters to Edisto Beach State Park, asking for permission to visit the park. Directed by the central office, the superintendent denied the request: "This park was established in 1935 for the exclusive use of white persons."

Three months later, the NAACP sued. By March 1956, with a federal judge on the verge of ruling against the state, the General Assembly, led by powerful Senator Marion Gressette, closed Edisto Beach State Park to the public and outlawed spending on desegregated facilities. The NAACP's lawsuit was dismissed on the grounds that Edisto Beach State Park was no longer open to whites or blacks. The park would remain closed for the next seven years.

A second lawsuit, Brown vs. S.C. State Forestry Commission, was filed in 1961 by NAACP lawyer Matthew Perry, who would later become South Carolina's first black federal judge. The suit alleged the state denied access to nine blacks at Myrtle Beach and Sesquicentennial state parks. On the heels of a city park desegregation

The native materials and simple architecture of this 1936-built footbridge in Paris Mountain State Park are exemplary of classic CCC style.

case in Memphis, federal Judge J. Robert Martin ruled against segregated parks in August 1963.

On the advice of Attorney General Daniel McLeod, the Forestry Commission agreed to close all 23 parks on September 8, 1963, before Martin's ruling went into effect. "I think it's a luxury we can dispense with rather than have integration thrust upon us," argued Senator Rembert C. Dennis of Berkeley County. The land of 16 of the parks that had been deeded to the state would revert to the original owners if the parks were ever abandoned. The state risked losing 24,000 acres—worth millions of dollars.

Time to "Do What Is Right"

Legislators argued that closing the parks reflected the will of the people and any attempt at integration would lead to violence. Those beliefs would soon be put to the test in a series of public hearings. Following Judge Martin's ruling, State Representative J. Clator Arrants of Kershaw County helped lead an informal referendum on the park closings. Few blacks attended the first hearings at the Greenville courthouse and Table Rock and Oconee state parks, but a surprising number of whites expressed moderate views on desegregation. Some speakers, such as the mayor of Walhalla, feared local economies would be hurt the most: "Take away Oconee State Park and take out the heart of Oconee County."

Segregationists dominated hearings in Barnwell, Beaufort and Edisto Beach, but park supporters turned out in force in Myrtle Beach, Cheraw, Chester, York and Columbia. Rock Hill schoolteacher Christine White warned that closing the parks would foster resentment in children. "In these days of racial tension, we must all endeavor to constantly do what is right," White wrote.

Open to All

Assured by state officials from Virginia and North Carolina that desegregation could be handled peacefully, Arrants' committee recommended reopening the parks to whites and blacks on a "limited basis."

The parks reopened on June 1, 1964,

and at the continued prodding of the public and Governor Robert McNair, the parks were fully operational and welcoming to all by the summer of 1966. No major incidents of violence were reported and, for the most part, blacks and whites continued to frequent the same segregated areas. Attendance once again was on the rise. With the support of citizens across the state, South Carolina's state parks had overcome their greatest challenge.

Looking to the Past

From their inception, the parks were meant to preserve South Carolina's history, and as early as the 1940s, the state had protected historical places such as the earthen fortifications at Rivers Bridge that mark the standoff between Confederate and Union troops. The state committed few resources and no full-time staff to historical sites until 1960 with the addition of Old Dorchester, the ruins of a Colonial-era village near Charleston, and Rose Hill, an elegant plantation home built in 1828.

In 1966, at the height of the historical preservation movement, Governor Robert McNair appointed the state's Tricentennial Commission to plan the celebration of the 300th anniversary of the state's first permanent European settlement at Charles Towne. The statewide event included three major expositions in Charleston, Columbia and Greenville. The Charleston expo would later become Charles Towne Landing, a state park with a full range of educational and interpretive exhibits on Colonial life. The Tricentennial attracted thousands of out-of-state tourists—even members of the British royal family. The state's historical places, charming antebellum homes and grand public buildings were finally seen as assets vital to South Carolina's fledgling tourism industry.

Parks, Recreation and Tourism

Governor McNair and state legislators realized the parks could play a role in promoting tourism, and it was time to end the state Forestry Commission's 33-year management of the parks. In 1967, the state's General Assembly created the South Carolina Department of Parks,

A TRADITION OF SERVICE

In 1946, U.S. Army veteran Ernest W. Cooler Jr. found a way to put his horticulture degree to work as the groundskeeper for the State House in Columbia. After a chance meeting with Forestry Commissioner Charlie Florey, he was offered a job at Hunting Island State Park. Soon, his younger brother, Norman, took over at Hunting Island after Ernest moved to Table Rock. By the 1950s, their brother Donald was on board at Edisto Beach State Park. Whenever the families went on vacation, they simply traded parks.

Norman Cooler made a career out of the park service, becoming the first Superintendent at Huntington Beach State Park in 1961, making the transition to Parks, Recreation & Tourism and ultimately serving as District Superintendent until his retirement. While Norman's two brothers left the parks to pursue other careers, the Cooler family produced two more generations of park employees.

"I know of at least six cousins who worked at the parks, and my son has worked there for the past three summers," said Ernest's son, Wes Cooler, a retired Marine and active supporter of conservation efforts along the Cherokee Foothills National Scenic Highway. "When I was 19, I spent the summer working for Uncle Norman at Huntington Beach, and I had a room in Atalaya. I was the only person living in a 52-room Moorish castle. I like to tell people I grew up in paradise."

In the past, Park Superintendents were jacks-of-all-trades. In 1998, the title was changed to Park Manager to reflect the need to supervise a wide range of activities. Park rangers receive law enforcement training, and other employees specialize in a wide range of responsibilities such as arborists, search and rescue, wildlife biology, event planning and business management.

Recreation & Tourism (PRT), led by an appointed commission made up of business leaders throughout the state. A year later, lawmakers approved a $6.25 million bond issue for park acquisition and new facilities. Over the next eight years, with millions of dollars in matching federal funds, PRT acquired land for 16 new parks and opened 12.

By the nation's Bicentennial celebration in 1976, South Carolina had acquired Landsford Canal on the Catawba River and Oconee Station, a frontier outpost; two antebellum mansions, Hampton Plantation and Redcliffe Plantation; and Musgrove Mill, the site of a bloody Revolutionary War battle.

Taming the Freshwater Coast

PRT now administered millions of dollars in federal Land and Water Conservation Funds and maintained the state's outdoor recreation plan. A major new thrust was boating and fishing along South Carolina's "freshwater coast." Beginning in 1954, the U.S. Army Corps of Engineers tamed the Savannah River with three major dams, creating 153,000 acres of freshwater lakes along the state's western border.

After the completion of Lake Hartwell in 1963 and Lake Russell in 1982, state parks offered some of the area's first public boat landings and campgrounds.

Six new parks opened on land leased from the Corps of Engineers — Lake Hartwell and Sadlers Creek on Lake Hartwell; Baker Creek, Hickory Knob and later Hamilton Branch on J. Strom Thurmond Lake; and Calhoun Falls on Lake Russell. After Duke Power Company built Lake Keowee, the company donated 1,000 acres to the state for Keowee-Toxaway. Under a lease agreement with South Carolina Electric & Gas, the state opened Dreher Island on Lake Murray. Later it purchased Lake Wateree State Park from Duke Power— ensuring public access and camping to many of South Carolina's major lakes.

In the early 1970s, PRT introduced new educational programs on trout fishing, bass fishing, fly-fishing and boating safety. "Our first major program was a trout fishing seminar at Oconee," recalled former State Parks Director Charles Harrison. "We brought in experts on trout fishing techniques, and about 150 people attended from at least nine states. It was even featured in *Southern Living* magazine. We were really among the first to offer these types of programs."

Back to Nature

Soon after PRT officials acquired the land for Jones Gap State Park, a wilderness area on the scenic Middle Saluda River, they were approached by the Greenville-based Naturaland Trust about plans to purchase Caesars Head.

Caesars Head is one of the state's most famous natural landmarks—a craggy, rock-faced cliff 3,266 feet above sea level (named either for the Roman emperor or for a previous owner's hunting dog). Naturaland Trust, led by Greenville attorney and outdoor enthusiast Tommy Wyche, proposed the protection of the 40,000-acre Mountain Bridge Wilderness Area that stretched from Table Rock to the Greenville County watershed, home to waterfalls, trails and more than 400 species of plants.

Over 10 years PRT worked with the group to create a protected corridor between Jones Gap and Caesars Head. Ultimately, the state spent $1.4 million, matched with nearly $5 million in federal funds and land donations to acquire the parks.

Two well-known holdouts were twin brothers from Greenville who owned Raven Cliff Falls, a breathtaking 420-foot series of cascades on the eastern rim of Caesars Head. The brothers refused to lower their price and claimed they were negotiating with Miami land developers to build a family resort there. They even talked about stringing a cable over the falls and charging for gondola rides to the top. Fear of losing the falls to development mobilized the public.

"Everybody tried to get these brothers to sell, and it was obvious they really enjoyed being courted," said former South Carolina Department of Parks, Recreation & Tourism Director Buddy Jennings, who oversaw engineering and planning at the time. "We met with Governor Dick Riley. He had proposed to his wife at Caesars Head,

One of the first, and still one of the most popular state parks, is the beachfront Myrtle Beach State Park.

A CASTLE FOR THE COAST

While they lived more than 1,000 miles away, Anna Hyatt and Archer Huntington were well-known South Carolina benefactors. Anna Hyatt was one of the nation's most prolific sculptors in bronze when she married New York philanthropist Archer Huntington in 1923. On a trip down South Carolina's coast in 1931, the Huntingtons fell in love with a 10,000-acre tract for sale between Myrtle Beach and Georgetown. Huntington bought the land to build his wife a studio, Brookgreen Gardens, and a winter home overlooking the sea called Atalaya.

Archer designed the home's Moorish architecture in his head. The centerpiece of the sprawling home was a tower that doubled as a cistern with a commanding view of the ocean. (Atalaya is Spanish for "watchtower.") Construction on the gardens and the home pumped badly needed dollars into the local economy during the Great Depression. Ten years later, the government occupied the home during World War II and set up a radar station. After the war, the Huntingtons only spent two more winters at Atalaya. The home's furnishings were removed after Archer Huntington's death in 1955. Five years later, the family leased the property to the state for Huntington Beach State Park.

Anna Hyatt Huntington continued to sculpt, and in 1967 she donated one of her last works to "the children of South Carolina"—a life-size bronze statue of a young Andrew Jackson riding bareback. Lancaster schoolteacher, Nancy Crockett, had mounted a letter-writing campaign to persuade Huntington to create it, and children across the region donated coins to pay for the statue's base—and install it in time to celebrate the 200th anniversary of Jackson's birth. Huntington died in 1973 at age 97, but her legacy lives on at Brookgreen Gardens, in the Andrew Jackson statue and in the annual fall art festival at Atalaya.

so he wanted us to try again. We told him we didn't think the brothers would ever sell unless we bought them a suitcase full of cash. We actually got approval to get the cash, but as it turned out we didn't need it. We were finally able to agree on a price, and they each donated about $200,000 of their proceeds."

Smiling Faces. Beautiful Places.

In addition to acquiring land, PRT officials were testing the waters of a new concept—the resort park. The resort park concept fit well with PRT's heightened focus on out-of-state tourism evident in the slogan developed by PRT's advertising agency: "South Carolina: Smiling Faces. Beautiful Places."

Hickory Knob included an 18-hole championship golf course, trails for hiking and biking, tennis courts, and facilities for archery and skeet shooting. The park offered cabins, a motel, restaurant and meeting facilities. At Santee, cabins were built on a pier extending into Lake Marion.

By the 1980s, federal support for state park projects had dried up. Years of expansion, including many special projects for local legislative delegations (such as the community swimming pool built next to the Rivers Bridge battlefield), had taken their toll on PRT's resources. Park staff was spread thin with little new money coming in.

To keep up with the workload, many park employees were working 70 hours a week. That changed when the South Carolina General Assembly approved 63 new positions. The first full-time naturalists were hired to support interpretive programs, and the overall professionalism of the parks improved.

Daylight After the Storm

In 1989, the state of South Carolina was hit by its worst natural disaster in modern times—Hurricane Hugo. The September storm raged ashore near Charleston with 137-mph winds and caused more than $4 billion in damage extending 200 miles inland. Hugo damaged park buildings and leveled thousands of trees, causing an estimated $4.5 million

in damage. Some staff, including Givhans Ferry Superintendent Glenn Farr, had opted to ride out the storm.

"I can tell you for sure we didn't know the fury we were facing," Farr wrote in the winter 1989 PRT newsletter. "Hugo didn't discriminate when it came to park trees. He didn't care whether you were a big tall pine or a big fat oak. You had to go. The sights all over the park were like a nightmare."

Hugo shut down 22 parks. It took nearly a year to reopen Charles Towne Landing. The ordeal, however, pulled the entire PRT team together with staff converging from across the state to repair the crippled parks. As the 1980s came to a close, the parks had overcome yet another major challenge. And a new vision was on the horizon.

Stewardship and Service

In the summer of 1987, a rag-tag group of river enthusiasts set out in canoes, kayaks and inner tubes from Colleton State Park for a 21-mile trip down the Edisto River to Givhans Ferry State Park. The fun-loving flotilla, known as Riverfest, drifted past remote tree-lined sections with overhanging Spanish moss and white limestone bluffs—scenes that have changed very little since American Indians first paddled the Edisto.

Riverfest, which celebrated its 21st anniversary in 2008, introduced thousands of outdoor enthusiasts to the serenity of South Carolina's blackwater rivers. Organizers created the Edisto River Canoe and Kayak Commission, which worked with landowners, state and federal agencies to create a nationally recognized canoe and kayak trail. As the Edisto River's popularity grew, the area experienced a tourism windfall.

"We've definitely seen an increase in tourism," said Charlie Sweat, an original Riverfest organizer who was later elected mayor of Walterboro. "Interstate 95 goes right through this area, so we even see people from out of state stopping over to explore the river."

With nature-based tourism on the rise in the 1990s, state parks focused on programs such as canoeing, hiking, back-country camping, bird watching and nature walking. Mountain biking trails were eventually opened at 12 parks. Croft State Park includes equestrian facilities and 21 miles of trails for horseback riding.

Another key initiative was the establishment of the Palmetto Trail, a 425-mile bicycling and walking trail that will link up the 85-mile Foothills Trail at Oconee State Park with the Swamp Fox Trail in the Francis Marion National Forest on the coast. Scheduled for completion in 2010, the Palmetto Conservation Foundation's Palmetto Trail will connect eight state parks, three national forests and many communities.

An increasing number of tourists are exploring South Carolina's rich history and culture. To capitalize on the heritage tourism trend, a grassroots effort supported by PRT led to the creation of the South Carolina Heritage Corridor. Designated by Congress as a National Heritage Area in 1996, it is one of only two dozen such designations in the nation. The corridor, which encompasses 18 state parks across 14 counties, runs from the foothills of Oconee County in the northwestern corner of the state to the port city of Charleston, and ties together historic buildings, museums, cultural activities and natural landscapes.

Conservation Outside the Parks

In fast-growing areas of the state, the rural countryside has been disappearing at an alarming rate and state parks in urban areas have become green oases. Sesquicentennial State Park is a perfect example. Once located in a remote area northeast of Columbia, the park is now surrounded by housing developments, movie theaters and shops.

In rural areas, proposals to build housing developments near state parks have been met with widespread opposition. Amid concerns about runoff and damage to the "view-shed," several local land trust groups have stepped up to protect these sensitive areas. In the mountains, S.C. 11 was designated as the Cherokee Foothills Scenic Highway, a 115-mile road that passes near six state parks.

New Vision

A move by the state General Assembly in 1993 to reorganize state government helped focus PRT's energies on the role and mission of the parks. Under the restructuring, the PRT Commission was dissolved and the PRT Director became a state cabinet-level position appointed by the governor. Under Grace Young, first cabinet director of PRT, an agency-wide planning team was formed to evaluate changes in recreation demand, as well as the public's expectations.

"It became obvious that the parks' mission had been poorly defined, had little focus and historically had responded arbitrarily to new recreational opportunities," recalled Mike Foley, retired chief of Resource Management. "We needed a plan to make the best use of our resources."

Under PRT's "New Vision" plan, the agency became the State Park Service and embraced two guiding principles—stewardship of the state's natural and cultural resources and service to South Carolina citizens and out-of-state visitors.

The plan called for a comprehensive inventory of plants, wildlife and historic sites. Parks were categorized by their unique features and usage. Some parks, including two of the original CCC parks, Chester and Barnwell, were designated as regional parks that would have programs geared toward the local community. Another class of parks, which includes Hickory Knob, Calhoun Falls and Lake Wateree, focuses on outdoor recreation, including fishing, boating and golfing.

Eight of the state's most popular parks—including Edisto Beach, Hunting Island, Huntington Beach, Kings Mountain, Myrtle Beach and Oconee—were designated as traditional parks. PRT began looking for ways to enhance these parks while maintaining their CCC-era look and feel. While cabins were updated with central air conditioning and modern appliances, the exteriors of the buildings retained their traditional look.

The Table Rock Lodge, which had been converted into a short-order restaurant in the 1960s, was painstakingly restored to its former grandeur. Supported by the Greenville business community, Paris

TOMMY WYCHE: BUILDING THE BRIDGE

Greenville's Tommy Wyche was an avid hiker and nature photographer in the 1970s when he started telling anyone who would listen about his dream to preserve the Mountain Bridge area. Ultimately, his skills as a lawyer would turn that dream into reality.

Wyche researched land holdings, lobbied for tax changes on conservation easements and devised complex land swaps with nonprofit groups to give landowners tax incentives to sell. Over 30 years, Wyche has worked with PRT and South Carolina Department of Natural Resources, the city of Greenville, Duke Energy, the Nature Conservancy and the Richard King Mellon Foundation to protect 60,000 acres of land, including two state parks. He was also a driving force behind the creation of 50 miles of trails that traverse the wilderness area, including the controversial suspension footbridge that crosses Raven Cliff Falls.

"A lot of people were worried the bridge would ruin the view of the falls," said Buddy Jennings, former Agency Director for PRT. "So Tommy agreed to build the bridge at his own expense, and he found volunteers to haul the timber and cables up to the falls. He told everyone that if it turned out to be an eyesore, he would take it down himself. That's just the kind of guy he is. As it turned out, the bridge is a major asset to that area."

LINDSAY PETTUS: STARTING WITH ONE ACRE

Lindsay Pettus, descendant of one of the state's first elected representatives, shares his ancestor's determination when it comes to land conservation. A frequent visitor to Landsford Canal State Park, Pettus was alarmed in 1995 when someone placed a trailer on 1.1 acres directly across the river from the interpretive trail for the park's 19th-century stone locks. Pettus contacted the landowner and offered to buy the property.

"That trailer was just being used as a hunting cabin, but it was just a real shame to have anything spoiling the view of the shoals," Pettus said. "The first thing I did was remove the trailer, but even before that, I was thinking, 'Now that I have this land, what am I going to do with it?' That's really why I formed the land trust."

Pettus' newly formed Katawba Valley Land Trust talked to Crescent Resources Inc. about buying an adjacent 209 acres on the river. PRT in 1998 acquired all 210 acres on the opposite shoreline. In 1998, the group secured 1,049 acres from Crescent Resources in Chester County. With the aid of U.S. Representative John Spratt and U.S. Senator Ernest Hollings, the federal government allocated $3 million in Legacy Forest funds to the state Department of Natural Resources, which manages the property. By 2007, the land trust had preserved more than 3,660 acres.

"We may have been the catalyst, but what we really did was put together quite a number of partnerships," Pettus said. "That's when you accomplish the most, when you can bring all the right people to the table, including, of course, the landowner."

Mountain's grand bathhouse was restored to its former glory and turned into a modern park center, complete with classrooms to support year-round education programs.

Sixteen parks were designated as special resource parks. The preservation of historical resources and delivery of educational programs are the primary thrusts at parks such as Charles Towne Landing, Oconee Station, Colonial Dorchester, and Hampton, Redcliffe and Rose Hill plantations. Certain parks were also recognized for their unique natural resources. Woods Bay State Natural Area, for example, preserves a mysterious topographic feature called a Carolina bay, an elliptical depression with a sandy rim that is always oriented toward the northwest.

Another special resource park, Landsford Canal State Park, rewards visitors with a variety of special features. Foremost, the canal's stone locks, lockkeeper's house, bridges and culverts tell the story of South Carolina's efforts in the 1820s to tame the Catawba River.

Landsford was once an important river crossing. But by the 20th century, the Catawba River was mostly enjoyed by local fishermen and the Catawba Indian potters who treasured the red clay in the riverbanks.

Today, Landsford Canal and its rocky shoals spider lilies draw thousands of lily watchers on the third Sunday in May. Recently bald eagle pairs have built nests along the shoals and still nest there.

Interpretation and Education

The Park Service developed interpretive programs supported by specialized staff to monitor and protect park resources. Dozens of tiny diamond-shaped signs on pine trees at Cheraw State Park mark the nests of threatened red-cockaded woodpeckers. Table Rock State Park, the state's only known site of breeding peregrine falcons, has participated in the annual Christmas bird count for a decade. And bird watchers have flocked to the overlook at Caesars Head for more than 20 years to view the fall hawk migration.

One of PRT's most successful interpretive programs focuses on threatened sea turtles which lay eggs in the sand dunes at four coastal parks. Each year, Edisto Beach State Park has one of the state's highest concentrations of sea turtle nests, often as many as 100 nests along the park's relatively short one-mile stretch of beach. Part of the turtles' success can be attributed to the park's aggressive public education programs.

"Whenever I speak to children, I point out that after these baby turtles leave Edisto Beach, they will return every year for 30 years to lay their eggs," Elaine Freeman, interpretive ranger at Edisto Beach said. "That's why we need to make sure they have a beach to return to, and when those children are grown up, they'll be able to do more than just tell their children about the turtles—they'll be able to bring them here and show them."

An increasing number of parks are supported by active volunteer groups. The Friends of Hunting Island has helped provide volunteer staff for tours of the historic lighthouse, plant sea oats along newly refurbished beaches and provide funding for new facilities and marsh boardwalks.

The Kings Mountain Living History Farm recreates the hard lives of Upstate farm families, from the blacksmith shed to the tiny wooden outhouse. Every December at Redcliffe Plantation State Historic Site, visitors are transported back to the Hammond family's 19th-century plantation for a unique program called "Christmas in the Quarters." In downtown Columbia, State Park Service tours of the State House feature the South Carolina Legislature in action, as well as the building's rich history, such as the stars on the western wall that mark the cannonball strikes from the Union army's siege of the city in 1865.

About 350,000 people participate in park interpretive programs each year, including 25,000 South Carolina school children. One of the major goals of PRT was the introduction of the Discover Carolina program, which under a partnership with Clemson University, provides first- through eighth-grade teachers an accredited program that integrates with school curriculums.

To make it easier to visit the parks, PRT introduced a central reservations system in 2005, eliminating the widely held practice of reserving campsites on a first-come, first-served basis. This simple innovation lets potential guests from anywhere in the world contact a single, toll-free telephone number or visit PRT's website to reserve any of the parks' 155 cabins, 80 motel rooms and 3,000 campsites.

Each year, an estimated nine million people enjoy South Carolina's state parks. Nearly one-third of those guests are out-of-state visitors, with a large majority coming from North Carolina and Georgia and some as far away as Canada. Surveys have shown that about half of South Carolina's adult population visits at least one state park a year. The Park Service manages 47 parks and eight historic properties encompassing more than 80,000 acres in every region of the state.

The Next Generation

Drawing on their 75-year heritage, South Carolina's state parks continue to support their original mission of promoting outdoor recreation while continuing to evolve to meet increased demand for activities such as mountain biking, bird watching and

personal watercraft. In 2006, the H. Cooper Black Field Trial Area near Cheraw became the state's 47th park. This highly specialized field trial course, developed by the state Forestry Commission, Department of Natural Resources and PRT, has an extensive trail system for horseback riders, fox hunt clubs and off-road vehicles.

Park management plans actively protect sensitive areas, using methods such as prescribed burning and selective thinning to promote biodiversity. Authenticity has become paramount at the state's historical sites. Under the $19 million remodeling project at Charles Towne Landing, historical documents and archaeological research helped rebuild the settlement's original log palisade wall. Archaeologists have unearthed the foundations of a structure built around 1670, making them among the oldest in America. The revitalization effort included the rebuilding of the *Adventure*, a full-size replica of a 17th-century ketch used for trading between ports in America and the Caribbean.

"Charles Towne Landing State Historic

Site is alive and well and now tells the story of the birth of South Carolina, indeed the American South, in a dynamic new fashion," said Edward "Buzzy" Tiencken, past president of the Friends of Charles Towne Landing. "Charles Towne Landing can now take its place with such national treasures as Jamestown as an example of how our birth as a nation should be preserved, interpreted and shared."

Even back in the 1930s, South Carolinians understood the need to protect the state's special places. As South Carolina's green space gradually gives way to urbanization, that job is becoming increasingly crucial.

"We've got a new generation of park personnel who must embrace our past while understanding the awesome responsibility of strategically managing for the future," said State Parks Director Phil Gaines. "Unless we're good stewards, these special places will be lost—along with pieces of who we are as South Carolinians. Our generation will be judged on what we deem as important to pass on to the next generation."

To experience firsthand the feel of the early state parks, simply book a stay in Cabin 6 at Oconee State Park. Built between 1935 and 1937, this native stone and wood structure is on the National Register of Historic Places.

The Parks

Park locations

The Coast

1. Charles Towne Landing State Historic Site
2. Colleton State Park
3. Colonial Dorchester State Historic Site
4. Edisto Beach State Park
5. Givhans Ferry State Park
6. Hampton Plantation State Historic Site
7. Hunting Island State Park
8. Huntington Beach State Park
9. Lake Warren State Park
10. Myrtle Beach State Park

The Midlands

11. Aiken State Natural Area
12. Andrew Jackson State Park
13. Baker Creek State Park
14. Barnwell State Park
15. Calhoun Falls State Recreation Area
16. Cheraw State Park
17. Chester State Park
18. Dreher Island State Recreation Area
19. H. Cooper Black, Jr. Memorial Field Trial and Recreation Area
20. Hamilton Branch State Recreation Area
21. Hickory Knob State Resort Park
22. Lake Greenwood State Recreation Area
23. Lake Wateree State Recreation Area
24. Landsford Canal State Park
25. Lee State Natural Area
26. Little Pee Dee State Park
27. Musgrove Mill State Historic Site
28. N.R. Goodale State Park
29. Poinsett State Park
30. Redcliffe Plantation State Historic Site
31. Rivers Bridge State Historic Site
32. Rose Hill Plantation State Historic Site
33. Santee State Park
34. Sesquicentennial State Park
35. Woods Bay State Natural Area

The Upstate

36. Caesars Head State Park/ Mountain Bridge Wilderness Area
37. Croft State Natural Area
38. Devils Fork State Park
39. Jones Gap State Park/ Mountain Bridge Wilderness Area
40. Keowee-Toxaway State Natural Area
41. Kings Mountain State Park
42. Lake Hartwell State Recreation Area
43. Oconee State Park
44. Oconee Station State Historic Site
45. Paris Mountain State Park
46. Sadlers Creek State Recreation Area
47. Table Rock State Park

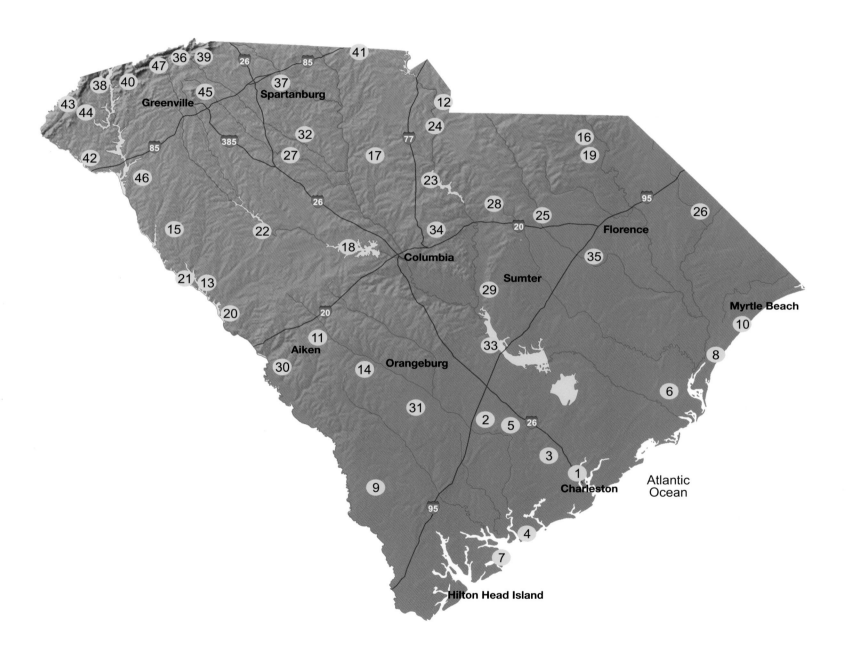

The Coast

*Sunrise on the beach,
Edisto Beach State Park*

Jumping dolphins can often be
spotted in the surf at Edisto Island.
But take time to look down. Edisto
Beach is one of the premier shelling
beaches on the Eastern Seaboard.

Remains of St. George's Anglican Church bell tower, Colonial Dorchester State Historic Site

Aboveground remains tell only part of the story. Beneath the ground are the remains of an entire town. Through active archaeological research, the State Park Service is working to unearth more of the mysteries of the underground buildings and artifacts of this important Colonial Era site.

Salt marsh, Edisto Beach State Park

Stately blue herons, tenacious woodpeckers and carefree otters are just some of the wildlife that greet visitors at Edisto Beach.

Early sunlight on the surf, Myrtle Beach State Park

The rolling surf at Myrtle Beach has been waking campers and welcoming day visitors since 1935. Myrtle Beach was the first state park to open in South Carolina.

Georgian Hampton Mansion, Hampton Plantation State Historic Site

Lessons learned in childhood stuck with George Washington even after he became President of the United States. On May 1, 1791, President Washington visited the Horry family at Hampton Plantation. Standing on the portico, Harriott Horry informed the President that she planned to remove an oak sapling that was growing directly in front of the portico. President Washington asked her to spare the tree. While legend holds that the infamous cherry tree fell to Washington's ax, the oak tree in front of the portico at Hampton Plantation still stands due to President Washington's pardon.

Diamondback terrapin, Hunting Island State Park

"Run Forrest, run." Many scenes from the blockbuster movie, *Forrest Gump*, were filmed in South Carolina's Lowcountry. Hunting Island was the main site of the Vietnam War scenes, including the widely recognized scene where Forrest carries his mortally wounded friend Bubba to the edge of a lagoon and holds him as he dies. Visitors to Hunting Island State Park often ask to see this exact spot.

Black bear, Charles Towne Landing State Historic Site

Bison, black bears and pumas were among the wildlife found at Charles Towne Landing in 1670 when the site was first settled by English traders and West-African slaves coming from Barbados. Today, the animal forest at Charles Towne Landing showcases these and other wildlife indigenous to the site.

Historic Hunting Island Lighthouse, Hunting Island State Park

The only lighthouse in South Carolina open to the public, Hunting Island Lighthouse is 167 steps to the top. If you're not winded from the climb, the view from atop will take your breath away.

Edisto River, Colleton State Park

Running from Edgefield and Saluda counties to Edisto Beach, the 206-mile-long Edisto River is one of the longest blackwater rivers in the United States. Blackwater rivers are characterized by their coffee color that comes from tannins leached from surrounding vegetation as the river moves through forested swamps and wetlands.

Palisade wall replica, Charles Towne Landing State Historic Site

English settlers and their West-African slaves came from Barbados to Albemarle Point at Charles Towne Landing in 1670. Facing the Ashley River, embrasures with mounted cannons protected them from attack by sea. A palisade wall protected them from attack by land.

Tidal foam, Myrtle Beach State Park

One of the rare pleasures of South Carolina's beaches is witnessing hatchling loggerhead sea turtles as they emerge from their beach nests and imprint the smooth morning sand. Programs at Myrtle Beach, Edisto Beach and Hunting Island state parks teach visitors about these fascinating creatures.

Spanish moss, Lake Warren State Park

Oak trees draped in Spanish moss evoke images of Scarlett O'Hara and Rhett Butler. Create memories of your own at Lake Warren State Park, a nationally recognized picnic area.

Marsh sunset, Hunting Island State Park

Looking at this photograph, one can inhale the distinctive scent of nutrient-rich pluff mud. Tidal marshes are critical to the ecology of the coast. But they also provide the raw materials for one of the South's highest art forms, Sweetgrass basket weaving, which was brought to South Carolina by West-African slaves. Today, Gullah descendants still weave baskets by hand.

Early morning light on Lake George Warren, Lake Warren State Park

South Carolina is home to over 450,000 acres of freshwater lakes. It's no surprise that South Carolina has more than 430,000 registered recreational watercraft (2008), one of the highest number per capita in the United States.

Atalaya Castle, Huntington Beach State Park

Built as a sculpture studio designed to hold live animals used as models, Atalaya Castle is a Moorish-inspired complex built by railroad heir Archer M. Huntington for his wife Anna Hyatt Huntington, a sculptor. Many of Mrs. Huntington's works can be seen at Brookgreen Gardens, located near the park. (See one of Mrs. Huntington's sculptures on page 59.)

Turkey vulture, Charles Towne Landing State Historic Site

In 1670, English settlers established the first permanent European settlement in the Carolinas at Charles Towne Landing. Today the park tells the story of the first settlers through its interactive "digital dig" archaeology exhibit, reproduction structures, replica sailing ships and living-history demonstrations. The plantation-era Legare-Waring House, also located at Charles Towne Landing, is available for weddings and special events. With its garden and approaching avenue of oaks, the Legare-Waring House provides a setting that is quintessentially Charleston.

Sea oats, Myrtle Beach State Park

Waves of charging dragonflies dart through the sea oats chirring and humming the shrill harmony of nature.

Beach sunrise, Huntington Beach State Park

From Blackbeard and his band of pirates to German U-Boats during World War II, the sea off of the coast of Huntington Beach State Park has hosted a variety of "guests," each part of the intriguing history of the South Carolina coast.

Great egret, Huntington Beach State Park

They originally planned the area as a private wildlife refuge. Huntington Beach's former owners Archer and Anna Hyatt Huntington created two freshwater impoundments to attract migratory waterfowl. More than 314 different species of birds have been sighted, making Huntington Beach one of the best destinations in the country for bird watchers.

Sunrise on the Atlantic surf, Edisto Beach State Park

"The sky is the daily bread of the eyes." —Ralph Waldo Emerson, from *Emerson's Journal*, May 18, 1843

Reflections in the blackwater of the Edisto River, Givhans Ferry State Park

Givhans Ferry was a crossing that connected the Old Indian Trail from Augusta, GA, to Charleston, SC. Named for a French Huguenot refugee who bought the land in 1777, it is believed that Phillip Givhan's home was burned by General Sherman in 1864 during the Civil War.

Live oak branches,
Myrtle Beach State Park

The Midlands

Carolina Yellow Jessamine, Baker Creek State Park

Found in all of South Carolina's 46 counties, the Carolina Yellow Jessamine is the state flower. "Legend of the Yellow Jessamine,"
a poem written in 1906 by Teresa Strickland, reads in part:

"No flower that blooms holds such perfume
As kindness and sympathy won.
Wherever there grows the sheltering pine
Is clinging a Yellow Jessamine vine."

"The Boy of the Waxhaws" sculpture by Anna Hyatt Huntington, Andrew Jackson State Park

The impetus for this sculpture, featured as the centerpiece of the celebration of the 200th anniversary of Andrew Jackson's birth, came from a sixth-grade class at Rice Elementary School in Lancaster, SC. The children wrote to Mrs. Huntington requesting that she sculpt a statue of young Jackson for the park. At age 90, Huntington obliged and in her letter to the class wrote: "A picture came to mind as I read over your letter ... I have Jackson as a young man of sixteen or seventeen seated bareback on a farmhorse, one hand leaning back on the horse's rump and looking over his native hill, to wonder what the future holds for him ...."

Lily pads in the Edisto River, Aiken State Natural Area

Comprised of four spring-fed lakes and the serpentine South Edisto River, Aiken State Natural Area is a combination of river swamp, bottomland hardwood forest and dry sandhill pine forest. The dry sandhill pine forest indicates a time when the sea reached to this westernmost portion of the state.

Reflections in Lake Russell, Calhoun Falls State Recreation Area

"There is a garden where our hearts converse
At ease beside clear water, dreaming
A whole and perfect future for yourself
Myself, our children and our friends."

—Theo Dorgan, from *The Promised Garden*

Canada geese, Chester State Park

Woody reflections in the lake, Sesquicentennial State Park

"The clearest way into the Universe is through a forest wilderness." —John Muir, American naturalist, author and founder of the Sierra Club

John of the Mountains: The Unpublished Journals of John Muir, Linnie Marsh Wolfe. ©1979 by the Board of Regents of the University of Wisconsin System. Reprinted by permission of The University of Wisconsin Press.

White-tailed deer, Dreher Island State Recreation Area

Centrally located on Lake Murray, Dreher Island is actually comprised of three islands connected by two bridges and one causeway. It is a popular spot for residents of South Carolina's Capital City/Lake Murray Country.

Cross-vine, Cheraw State Park

Established in 1934, Cheraw is the oldest state park in South Carolina. Local citizens and schoolchildren raised funds to purchase the initial site. Over the years, the park has grown to 7,361 acres.

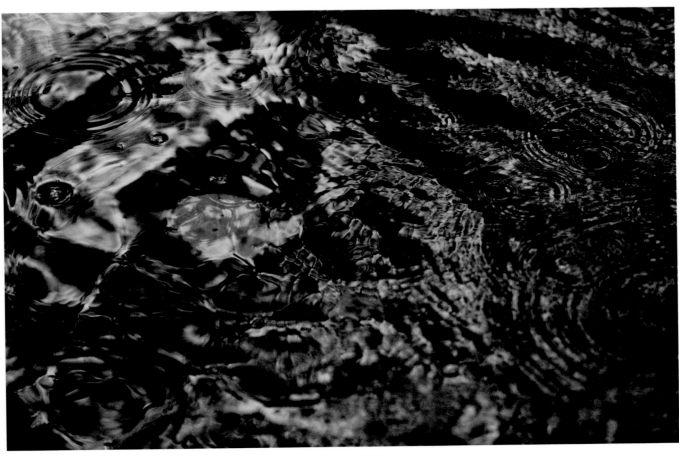

Autumn leaf, Barnwell State Park

Barnwell State Park is named for Colonel John Barnwell, a surveyor and one of the first settlers on Port Royal Island. Also known as "Tuscarora Jack," he led successful campaigns against the Tuscarora and Yamassee Indians in the early 1700s and formed the Carolina Scouts, a waterborne militia that patrolled the inland passage between Charleston, SC, and St. Augustine, FL.

Reflections in the cypress-tupelo swamp, Woods Bay State Natural Area

Carolina bays, large eliptical depressions in the ground, are unique geological features. The mystery of their origin remains unresolved.

Osprey with prey, Santee State Park

Perched on Lake Marion, Santee State Park is a popular launch for fishermen wishing to tap the congregation of fish in the lake. Part of the Santee Cooper Lakes, Lake Marion is one of the few man-made lakes with a self-sustaining striped bass population. These lakes cover more than 170,000 acres and are also known for large and abundant catfish.

Canopy of the pine forest, Hickory Knob State Resort Park

In addition to serene beauty, Hickory Knob State Resort Park offers a one-of-a-kind experience featuring camping, cabins, motel rooms and a Tom Jackson-designed golf course. It is an affordable option for family reunions or group retreats.

Moonrise, Lake Greenwood State Recreation Area

An unfinished rock wall at the entrance to Lake Greenwood has stood for years as reminder of the sacrifices made when men were quickly called to arms during World War II. The Civilian Conservation Corps workers who built the park were no exception as they put down their tools and went to defend our country.

Pine forest, Chester State Park

"Imagination, new and strange
In every age, can turn the year;
Can shift the poles and lightly change
The mood of men, the world's career."

—John Davidson, from *Imagination*

Rocky shoals spider lilies in the Catawba River, Landsford Canal State Park

"When ... the rocky shoals spider lily is in bloom, they provide one of the grandest natural history sights in the southeastern United States." —Rudy Mancke, Naturalist and host of SCETV's *NatureScene*

Sunset over Lake Juniper, Cheraw State Park

"Every day is a new beginning, and every sunset is merely the latest milestone on a voyage that never ends." —Ronald Reagan

Reprinted by permission of The Ronald Reagan Presidential Foundation.

Pointer at Bird Dog Field Trial, H. Cooper Black, Jr. Memorial Field Trial and Recreation Area

Catering to equestrian and retriever/sporting dog events, the park is named in memory of H. Cooper Black, Jr., MD, a Columbia surgeon and outdoor enthusiast.

Wisteria amid the dogwood blooms, Lake Greenwood State Recreation Area

Wisteria and blooming dogwood trees are two sure indicators of spring in South Carolina, providing some of the earliest punches of color and beckoning the many fruits of spring and summer.

J. Strom Thurmond Lake, Hickory Knob State Resort Park

There are a variety of modern accommodations available to visitors of Hickory Knob State Resort Park. But the most unique experience is a night in the historic Guillebeau House. The Guillebeau House was constructed around 1770 in the Huguenot settlement of New Bourdeaux, which is near the park. The house was relocated to the park and restored in 1983. It is available for overnight rental.

Historic lane of magnolia trees, Redcliffe Plantation State Historic Site

This lane of magnolia trees defines a tunnel of time that takes us through four generations, black and white, who lived, worked and died at Redcliffe Plantation. Their collective efforts molded the natural environment at Redcliffe over many difficult years.

Spider lily reflected in the Catawba River, Landsford Canal State Park

"Oh, give us pleasure in the flowers today;
And give us not to think so far away
As the uncertain harvest; keep us here
All simply in the springing of the year."

—Robert Frost, from *A Prayer in Spring*

Cormorants, N.R. Goodale State Park

The 140-acre lake at **N.R.** Goodale State Park is the byproduct of a Civil War Era mill. It now provides a habitat for many bird species, including a great blue heron rookery.

Sunrise over Lake Wateree, Lake Wateree State Recreation Area

Lake Wateree is South Carolina's oldest hydroelectric lake. The lake contains more fish per acre than any other lake in the state.

Spring reflections, Cheraw State Park

Home to many different species of plants, Cheraw is a masterpiece of nature during the spring.

Redbuds in spring, Calhoun Falls State Recreation Area

Calhoun Falls State Recreation Area includes a marina, giving boaters access to the clear water of Lake Russell.

Sunrise over J. Strom Thurmond Lake, Hamilton Branch State Recreation Area

Rocky shoals spider lily, Landsford Canal State Park

"The scenery here cannot fail to interest. Ten thousand rocks and grassy islets meet the traveler's eye, ten thousand murmuring streams meander through them." —Robert Mills, noted architect from South Carolina and designer of Landsford Canal, describing the area in 1826. Mills also designed the Washington Monument.

Mud snake, Lee State Natural Area

During the construction of Lee State Natural Area, several Civilian Conservation Corps workers who hailed from South Carolina's Lowcountry got homesick. As a remedy, they took three trucks to Charleston and collected Spanish moss, which is found hanging from trees in the Lowcountry. Now more than 75 years later, Spanish moss is still flailing in the wind as it hangs from trees at Lee.

Water-shield in the Little Pee Dee River, Little Pee Dee State Park

Scenes like this make one wonder if Monet ever visited South Carolina.

Reflections in J. Strom Thurmond Lake, Hamilton Branch State Recreation Area

"... I come into the presence of still water.
And I feel above me the day-blind stars
waiting with their light. For a time
I rest in the grace of the world, and am free."

—Wendell Berry, from "The Peace of Wild Things"

Cypress canoe trail, N.R. Goodale State Park

"Nature does not hurry. Yet everything is accomplished." —Lao Tzu

Artesian springs, Lee State Natural Area

Renewal is a characteristic often associated with water. The natural environment witnessed all over South Carolina, and embodied in state parks, refreshes one's soul and mind like no other elixir.

Horseshoe Falls, Musgrove Mill State Historic Site

During the summer of 1780, as British troops occupied the Musgrove family home on the Enoree River, Mary Musgrove acted as a Patriot spy. Mary, daughter of the property's owner, took great risks to support the Revolution. She hid one Patriot soldier underneath the falls. The soldier, known as Horseshoe Robinson, is the namesake of what is now Horseshoe Falls.

Wisteria blossoms among pinecones, Little Pee Dee State Park

Nature's random combinations of coarse and delicate, heavy and light, create a depth of interest that can't be replicated inorganically.

Salkehatchie River, Rivers Bridge State Historic Site

During the Civil War, a Union officer referred to the Salkehatchie River as "this indescribably ugly Salkehatchie." However, the area provided a key defense for Confederate troops.

Mansion and rose gardens, Rose Hill Plantation State Historic Site

Rose gardens dot the landscape of this cotton plantation once owned by former South Carolina Governor William Henry Gist. A reputed duelist, Gist is also known for his challenge to Union authority after the election of Abraham Lincoln making him the "Secession Governor."

Mountain laurel, Poinsett State Park

The topography of Poinsett State Park represents the intersection of South Carolina's coastal plain and midlands sandhills. Steep hills and bluffs provide the background for an unusual mix of plants and animals. Strange sights such as mountain laurel festooned with Spanish moss are common at Poinsett.

Enoree River, Musgrove Mill State Historic Site

"We must use time creatively, in the knowledge that the time is always ripe to do right. Now is the time to make real the promise of democracy and transform our pending national elegy into a creative psalm of brotherhood. Now is the time to lift our national policy from the quicksand of racial injustice to the solid rock of human dignity." —Martin Luther King, Jr., from "Letter from Birmingham Jail," April 16, 1963

Bald cypress, Woods Bay State Natural Area

Walk through the cypress-tupelo swamp on the 500-foot boardwalk at Woods Bay State Natural Area, where more than 75 species of mammals, reptiles and amphibians, along with 150 species of birds, can be found.

Great egret, Santee State Park

Often standing motionless to await its prey in shallow water, the statuesque great egret, also known as the white heron, inhabits wetlands and shallow waters in many parts of South Carolina.

Bracken ferns, Dreher Island State Recreation Area

Sited along the banks of Lake Murray, one of the best-known largemouth and striped bass fishing destinations in the South, Dreher Island State Recreation Area is the perfect place to launch a boat for a day of fishing.

Pine and hardwood forest, Poinsett State Park

"I like trees because they seem more resigned to the way they have to live than other things do." —Willa Cather, 1913

Live oaks, Sesquicentennial State Park

This stand of live oaks evokes images of a bygone era. But Sesquicentennial State Park, an urban oasis in Columbia, offers contemporary facilities such as a certified ropes team-training course and a "bark park" designed for canine visitors and their human friends.

Greek revival porch of Redcliffe Mansion, Redcliffe Plantation State Historic Site

"We have to do with the past only as we can make it useful to the present and to the future." —Frederick Douglass,
from *What to the Slave is the Fourth of July?*

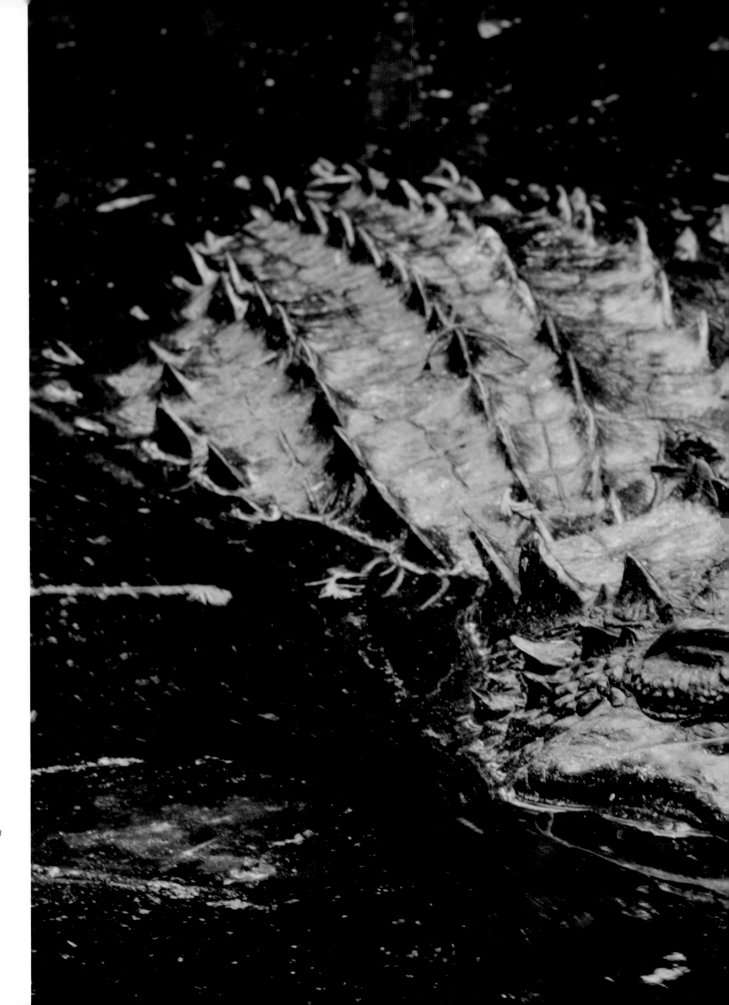

Alligator in the Carolina bay,
Woods Bay State Natural Area

The Upstate

Autumn view toward Table Rock,
Caesars Head State Park/
Mountain Bridge Wilderness Area

Sunflower, Lake Hartwell State Recreation Area

"Nature's first green is gold,
 Her hardest hue to hold.
 Her early leaf's a flower;
 But only so an hour.
 Then leaf subsides to leaf.
 So Eden sank to grief,
 So dawn goes down to day.
 Nothing gold can stay."

—Robert Frost, *Nothing Gold Can Stay*

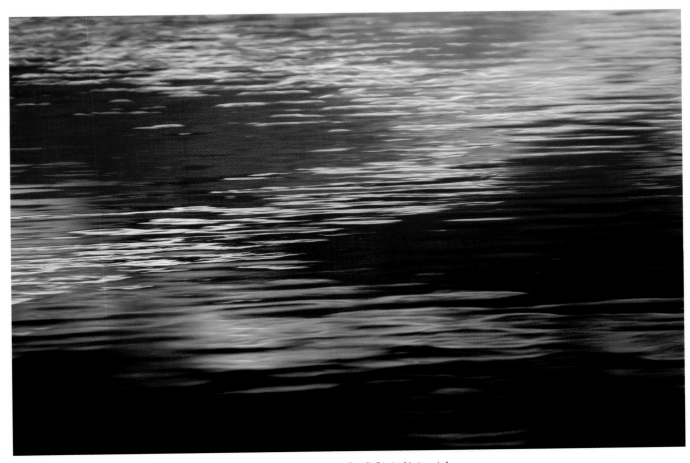

Sunset on Lake Craig, Croft State Natural Area

"Nature rarer uses yellow
 Than another hue;
 Saves she all of that for sunsets, –
 Prodigal of blue,
 Spending scarlet like a woman,
 Yellow she affords
 Only scantly and selectly,
 Like a lover's words."

—Emily Dickinson, *Nature Rarer Uses Yellow*

Lake Jocassee, Devils Fork State Park

Jocassee Gorge holds the deep, cool waters of Lake Jocassee. Trout fishing is a popular activity on this 7,500-acre reservoir, which runs as deep as 350 feet. Hear the cascading waterfalls, view bald eagles and peregrine falcons in flight, or enjoy spring as the rhododendrons and rare Oconee Bell bloom. Devils Fork State Park, the only public park on Lake Jocassee, is located off of Cherokee Foothills National Scenic Highway SC 11.

Red maple leaves, Keowee-Toxaway State Natural Area

Experience views of the Blue Ridge and visit the museum at Keowee-Toxaway State Natural Area. The museum tells the story of the Cherokee people and their complex relationship with European settlers.

Frontier home, Oconee Station State Historic Site

The William Richards House served as a residence and frontier trading post in the early 1800s. At the time, the area was considered to be the end of civilization. Those who wandered beyond Oconee Station were on their own in the wilderness frontier. Today, the nearby Oconee State Park serves as the southern trailhead for the Foothills Trail, an 80-mile path on the Blue Ridge Escarpment leading to Table Rock Mountain.

American crow, Sadlers Creek State Recreation Area

"See how willingly Nature poses herself upon photographers' plates. No earthly chemicals are so sensitive as those of the human soul. All that is required is exposure and purity of material." —John Muir

Oconee bells, Devils Fork State Park

"I am following Nature without being able to grasp her, I perhaps owe having become a painter to flowers." —Claude Monet

Sweetgum leaves and branches, Kings Mountain State Park

Kings Mountain State Park is adjacent to Kings Mountain National Military Park, site of an important American victory during the Revolutionary War. The October 7, 1780 victory was the first major Patriot victory after the British invasion of Charleston in May 1780. Trails connect the two parks.

Raven Cliff Falls, Caesars Head State Park/Mountain Bridge Wilderness Area

A thread of mountain water cascades more than 400 feet, crashing into Matthews Creek at Raven Cliff Falls, one of the most often-hiked waterfall trails in South Carolina. For a different perspective, view Raven Cliff Falls from the viewing platform at Caesars Head in the Mountain Bridge Wilderness Area. (An alternate view from the same platform is pictured on pages 108 and 109.)

Early autumn, Keowee-Toxaway State Natural Area

"Nature is a mutable cloud which is always and never the same." —Ralph Waldo Emerson, from "History"

Replica 1800s farm, Kings Mountain State Park

Kings Mountain State Park features a popular living history farm where visitors can learn about how a typical Piedmont farm functioned in the mid-1800s. Interpreters provide demonstrations of daily farm life at the replica house, gin and barn.

Fog and mist, Jones Gap State Park/Mountain Bridge Wilderness Area

South Carolina's first designated scenic river, the Middle Saluda River, flows through Jones Gap State Park providing habitat for native-born wild trout, including the rare Brookie. An on-site environmental education center and restored portions of the historic Cleveland Fish Hatchery provide a laboratory for ecological research and education.

Jocassee Gorges, Devils Fork State Park

"A lake is the landscape's most beautiful and expressive feature. It is earth's eye; looking into which the beholder measures the depth of his own nature." —Henry David Thoreau, from *Walden*

Woodland ferns, Croft State Natural Area

"Look deep into nature, and then you will understand everything better." —Albert Einstein

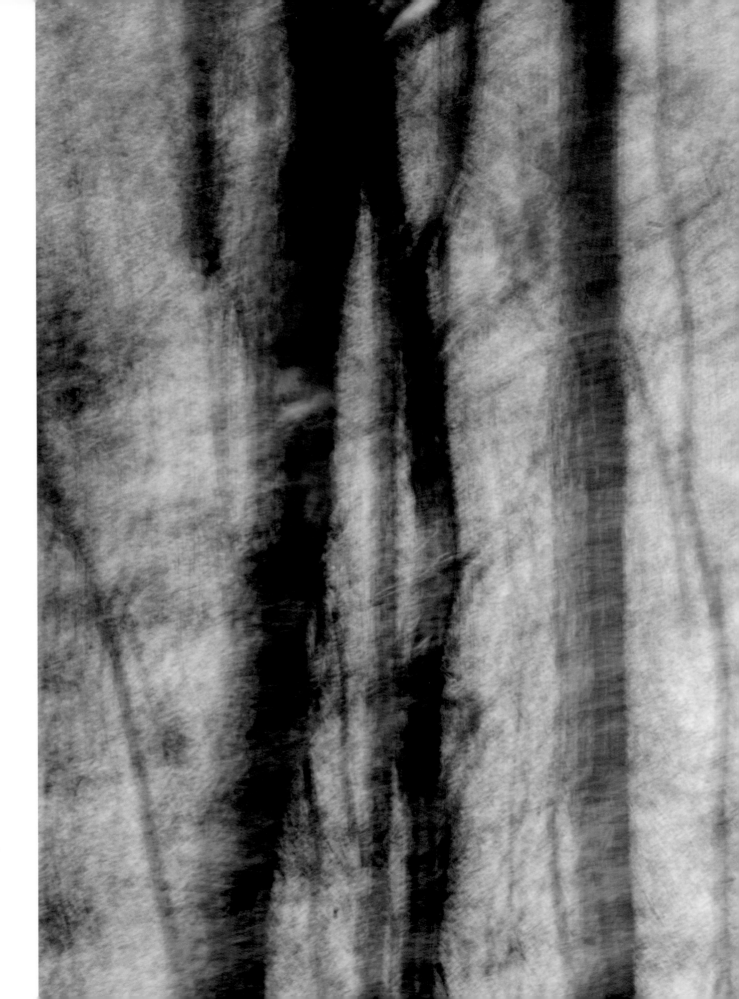

Snow on the forest floor,
Table Rock State Park

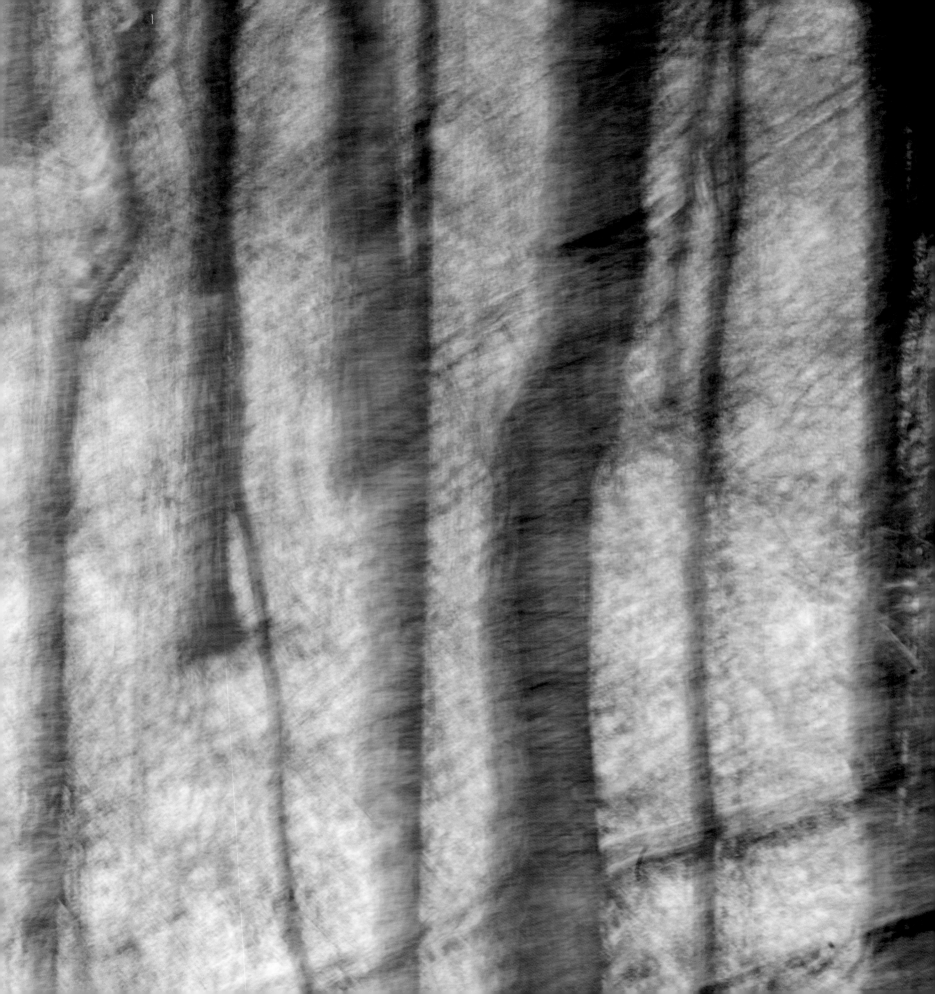

Sunrise over the Blue Ridge Escarpment, Jones Gap State Park/Mountain Bridge Wilderness Area

Jones Gap and Caesars Head state parks form the Mountain Bridge Wilderness Area, an 11,000-acre quilt of mountain woodlands on the Blue Ridge Escarpment.

Colors of the season, Devils Fork State Park

In the South, fall is notable for reasons as varied as the beginning of college football season to pecan harvesting. But along the Cherokee Foothills National Scenic Highway in South Carolina's Upstate, colors emerge changing the landscape into nature's short-lived fireworks display.

Fall foliage, Oconee State Park

When the air cools, warblers and songbirds return to herald the start of fall birding season at Oconee State Park. Other unique seasonal sights at the park include ladies and gentlemen dressed in square dancing regalia. Square dancing is a long-standing summertime activity at the Oconee barn.

Sunset from Caesars Head, Caesars Head State Park|Mountain Bridge Wilderness Area

Some see the head of Caesar in the unique granite outcropping that sits atop the Blue Ridge Escarpment at Caesars Head State Park. However you interpret the shape of the outcropping, Caesars Head is a must-see attraction in South Carolina's Upstate.

Waterfowl, Sadlers Creek State Recreation Area

Observe the amplitude of wildlife at Lake Hartwell. Sadlers Creek State Recreation Area sits on a peninsula stretching into the lake, a 56,000-acre reservoir for the Savannah River.

Lake Oolenoy surrounded by autumn color, Table Rock State Park

Completely restored in 2005, the lodge at Table Rock State Park is a popular location for weddings and events. The structure, which was originally built by the Civilian Conservation Corps in 1940, is listed on the National Register of Historic Places. From the lodge, visitors have an awe-inspiring view of Table Rock Mountain.

Hardwood forest, Paris Mountain State Park

Now a treasured green space in the midst of fast-growing Greenville, Paris Mountain State Park was once a rural retreat.
A bathhouse from the 1930s has been recently restored. It houses historical exhibits and a 3-D map of the mountainside park.

Waters of Lake Hartwell, Sadlers Creek State Recreation Area

"I hear lake water lapping with low sounds by the shore ... I hear it in the deep heart's core." —William Butler Yeats, from "The Lake of Innisfree"

Shadows on rock, Table Rock State Park

"This our life, exempt from public haunt, finds tongues in trees, books in the running brooks, sermons in stones, and good in every thing." —William Shakespeare, from *As You Like It*

Black gum leaves, Lake Hartwell State Recreation Area

"In every walk with nature one receives far more than he seeks." —John Muir

Maple leaf, Oconee State Park

"What does he plant who plants a tree?
 He plants cool shade and tender rain,
 And seed and bud of days to be,
 And years that fade and flush again;
 He plants the glory of the plain;
 He plants the forest's heritage;
 The harvest of a coming age;
 The joy that unborn eyes shall see –
 These things he plants who plants a tree."

—Henry Cuyler Bunner, from *The Heart of the Tree*

Pinxter flower in bloom, Paris Mountain State Park

The spray of spring flowers emerging, the racing stripes of competitive bicyclists, and the red and green of Boy Scout uniforms at Camp Buckhorn are all sights at Paris Mountain State Park.

*Rushing mountain streams,
Keowee-Toxaway
State Natural Area*

Artist's Statement

"Mountain magic." You will understand this phrase if you have ever escaped the world of electronics, concrete and steel to camp under a waning moon with the river singing among the shadows of the Blue Ridge. Staring in awe at a summer sunset song on the coast of Carolina with the thunderous rolling of the tide, I found myself reconnecting with the earth. The mountains, piedmont and coast have nourished my spirit while I worked on this book project, sharing with me the beauty of this world, the honesty of nature and the intricate web of life that encompasses us all. The mountains become part of the sea, the sea a part of the desert, and the desert an oasis in itself to another form of life, and I understand that our future lies within the wisdom of the earth.

I feel blessed to have experienced every state park in South Carolina while working on this project. Let me say from firsthand experience, the beauty of South Carolina is right outside your back door. The parks are an incredible resource with giving and caring people to make the experience more enjoyable. I hope you and your family will take a day, a week or just an hour to spend time together celebrating and exploring the beauty of South Carolina State Parks.

To the South Carolina parks staff: you are the gate-keepers and guardians of a resource that is irreplaceable. The parks themselves are a true blessing to the people of South Carolina and those just passing through. Both the people and the parks are making this world a better place. Words alone cannot express my gratitude. Thank you.

all the best,
jon holloway

Rock outcroppings, Jones Gap State Park/Mountain Bridge Wilderness Area